World Government Manifesto 2

By: Madison
Stahurski-Dunstall

certain other
noncommercial uses
permitted by copyright
law.

ISBN: 9781304619761

Table of contents

Values and ideals in this society

Specialization, technology and space

Language and architecture

The way humans will look, their gender and sexual orientation

Indigenous rights and people outside the circles

Conclusion

Introduction

This manifesto/book will discuss world government and what I think it should be like. World government is one government instead of having multiple governments and nation states. A world government would mean no more nation states and countries but one whole united earth.

System of government

There are many different systems of government but in this world government, I think augmented democracy would work best. Augmented democracy is a form of direct democracy by using a digital avatar to vote. This virtual avatar would be using artificial intelligence through personal questions and situations and ideas to determine how that person would vote, it would automatically vote unless you turn it off for a specific vote that you want to vote on and if you look at votes and are not seeing how you would vote, you can do some more quizzes and even though you can't change your vote, you can say that's not how you would have voted

4

so the AI can learn.
Each person has one
vote and everything
would result in a
majority,
since the whole
population of the world
would be voting, I
would not think there
would be a tie but if
there was, the bill or
whatever is being
voted one will become
invalidated and would
have to be
reprocessed if

someone wants that bill or whatever to pass. Since not everyone will have sufficient knowledge on all topics. There will be a board of specialists voted in each section by their like minds. So any agricultural person will be qualified and will all vote for the one person they want to represent them. They will have 5 vetoes and even though anyone can propose a bill or resolution or whatever. The committee of specialists will be mostly trying to propose bills and rallying for them and lobbying for them. This may be seen as technocratic but people who are the best in their field should have a bigger say since they probably know what's best. More will be discussed later on

birthing and education
but there will be an
overseer to make sure
everyone is doing their
jobs and their system
is working properly
and no corruption is
taking place. There
will be a lottery at birth
for babies with certain
qualities found out
through genetic testing
to be great leaders
and one will be
chosen which will be
taught since birth how
to do this job. The first

one will probably be
voted in and one they
reach 50, a new
candidate will be
chosen and will
replace then after they
die or if they are
deemed unfit to lead.
They will have an
accompanying team
that apply and are
chosen based on their
qualifications to help
guide them and to
help keep an eye on
things and report to
the leader. One thing

many people do not
know is that the United
States founders but
safeguards against too
much democracy as
they saw it as bad and
I think this is quite
similar since
sometimes the people
do
not know what is best
and I have always
loved modern
monarchies and I think
a person who is not
truly involved but
advising and

overseeing is important to healthy society. This system of government will be fair where everyone will get a vote except those in the above mentioned leadership positions so it is fair but we need specialists and a leader to make sure everything is going well and to make sure we are doing the right and best thing, there will be no provinces, states or even cities. Every law and decision is applied the same throughout the world so everyone around the world participates and is treated the same. There will be no by-laws and no worrying about different laws in different areas.Instead of direct democracy, augmented democracies uses intelligent software agents that participates on a humans behalf in e-rulemaking processes. The problem is current social bot technology is not up to that task as they are not sufficiently sophisticated enough. This would also need a reliable authentication mechanism to enable agencies to distinguish between legitimate bots or malicious ones (Perez, 2020). A definiton of technocracy is people in power due to their technical knowledge. The mentality of technocrats is that they have a skepticism of political institutions as well as politicians, preference for being pragmatic instead of moral or ideological, confidence that problems can be solved through technological or scientific method, do not care for sympathy or openness of democracy and wanting technological progress in the form of material productivity while not caring about social justice or distribution. It is important for all societies to have sectoral or limited technocracies in regard to physicians, civil engineers and military. These are the accepted ones but unaccepted ones are agricultural researchers, evolutionary biologists and climate scientists. Socialism and technocracy is connected since they both value science and technology. Piecemeal social engineering is introducing rational approbate reforms into society and then undertake evidence based assessments

(Yongmou, 2016). The benefits of constitutional democracies is that today, many prosperous countries such as Canada, Britain and Japan have a prosperous and peaceful state. Constitutional monarchies are better at protecting property rights of both individuals and businesses. Countries with both a president

and prime minister
end up in power
struggles between the
offices or they usurp
democratic rights
together
such as Russia and
Türkiye. It is more of a
ceremonial role and
the office is anchored
in tradition and
continuity (The, 2023).

References

Oren Perez. 2020. Collaborative e-Rulemaking, Democratic Bots, and the Future of   Digital Democracy. Digit. Gov.: Res. Pract. 1, 1, Article 8 (January 2020), 13 pages. https://doi.org/ 10.1145/3352463

The, E. B. (2023). *Boring is beautiful: The quiet benefits of*

Canada's constitutional monarchy: Many of the most prosperous, stable and progressive countries in the world today have hereditary monarchs that serve as their heads of state. The Globe and Mail.

Yongmou, L. (2016). The Benefits of Technocracy in China. *Issues in Science and Technology, 33*(1), 25-28.

Rearing and education

In this world, rearing and education would be a lot different, for the greater good. I am hoping technology will start to develop enough to have artificial wombs so we don't need to worry about procreation anymore. The children will be genetically altered to be the best of themselves and

when they are born,
they will be raised to
what they need
individually and will be
raised in groups by
humans with the help
of AI and robots.
Social interaction and
bonding will be
important but they will
be raised to love and
believe in collectivity
and the greater good.
They will be raised
compassionately and
very freely to express
themselves how they

want in lines of reason
and safety. Children
will be medically dealt
with well and
supervised constantly
to make sure
they are okay. They
will be tested
constantly to
understand what they
need best. Their
education will be very
individualized with
exploring a wide
breach of subjects but
also focusing on the
fundamentals, this will

be the way the world
and once they choose
what they want to do,
their training will be
focused on just that till
they are ready to enter
the workforce. Their
will be no money but
there will be a social
credit system. They
will be able to get
everything they need
as long as they are a
good person and
citizen to the world,
there will always be
lifelong learning and if

they want a new career, they can transfer to what they want to do after the proper training. This will be a world of limitless opportunity and there will be a great support system and everyone will be the best they can be.

Currency and needs/wants

There will be no currency as we know it today. There will be no money but there will be a social credit system. I am basing this off of what China has. Everyone in the world will have basic needs for survival. The social credit system is for wants. This will encourage people to be good citizens by monitoring what they do and how they interact with people to determine their score and based on their score, they can have extra privileges. This system is to keep everyone in check and to make sure society and everyone functions the best they can to have a good and healthy society,The Indian government has a project to have a database containing its populations biometric and demographic data. It has been said to be a very sophisticated ID program. This project has been criticized as being a danger to Indians citizens privacy. The project is called Aadhaar and it is a voluntary project to help with convenience. This is criticized as being voluntary as you need to enrol to have access to financial and social services. The Social Credit System in China is similar but it also uses information it collects to predict things like paying off mortgages and credit card bills. These systems come from the big data belief that this will help end a lot of problems plaguing society such as violence, corruption and even market crashes. An unofficial program was by the United States that Edward Snowden whistleblower on where the US government was running surveillance programs on its citizens and around the world. There is also the techno utopian view that big data is untainted and objective of human foibles. This idea also holds the value that people are responsible for their privacy and not governments or corporations. There is also the concern of corporations working with government like how Edward Snowden explained the US government colluded with major corporations like Apple. Aadhar collects fingerprints and iris information. Commercial enterprises would benefit from Aadhaar with the Know Your Customer, KYC, is a regulation that allows financial instituons allowing to possess personal details of their clients. Many business would be bale to meet the KYC regulation and it will simplify tac collection as well as transactions and payments. This system will also remove the middlemen which will help reduce corruption. This is for pension payments and also subsidized rates for food or certain products. For the SCS, citizens and businesses, especially small businesses, would benefit from it. The Chinese got their idea from the American system of using a credit score to base whether people can get loans and mortgages (Shahing & Zheng, 2020)."

References

Shahin, S., & Zheng, P. (2020). Big Data and the Illusion of Choice: Comparing the Evolution of India's Aadhaar and China's Social Credit System as Technosocial Discourses. Social Science Computer Review,

38(1), 25-41.
https://doi.org/
10.1177/0894439
318789343

Security

In this world, every city would essentially be a smart city. This would mean high security, everything videotaped and monitored by a high tech AI with facial recognition and the best tech has to offer. This will work hand in hand with the social credit system, this will all be connected to a system run by AI and people to make sure the world is amazing, everyone is safe. This system will try to predict people based on all the information it collects which will be everything. This will be used for each person who will have access to themselves to see what it thinks and hopefully help them make good decisions. This will also be used in the world government to make sure the world is safe and to identify threats at The present and in the future. This will be a world where everyone is educated on this and people will be educated to know this is what's best for them in the collectivistic and utilitarian society. This will hopefully allow people to feel safe and secure knowing they and others are being watched. If you don't know, utilitarianism is a theory based on doing what is good for the collective. For example, sacrifice the one to save the many. This will be one of the core philosophies of this society which is putting the greater good above anyone else and I hope that anyone in this society would risk their lives for this ideal.

The use and idea of CCTV is a deterrence

to criminals since it provides a greater risk of detection and then arrest. CCTV has also grown in its use and technological capability. CCTV is generally seen as a great deterrent in the first few months until criminals learn the camera placements and how to avoid them. To prevent crime, it is thought the offender has to be aware a mare is monitoring their activity and the crime is not work the risk of being caught by the police Ratcliffe et al, 2009). This data did not include facial recognition in CCTV or having CCTV everywhere. There is also a difference between using cameras that can be directly seen from a station or where you have to download the camera footage or be

in close viscinity to it
(Ratcliffe et al, 2009).

References

Jerry H. Ratcliffe, Travis Taniguchi & Ralph B. Taylor (2009) The Crime Reduction Effects of Public CCTV Cameras: A Multi-Method Spatial Approach, Justice Quarterly, 26:4, 746-770, DOI: 10.1080/0741882 0902873852

**Living and if anyone
is forced to live in
that society**

This world will have a
smart circle
everywhere, this will
be like the line
proposed in Saudi
Arabia. These smart
circles will be
specialized as for
example,
agricuturalists will all
live together which will
help with elected
leaders and to make

more productive work with everyone working together and children will even have their own smart circle until they are old enough to choose their path and go to a smart circle for where they want to work. These circles will hopefully be everywhere and will provide everything the people need, the only reason to travel is in case you want to visit historical artifacts or meet other people. To travel, it will be by AI powered planes/ helicopters with of course humans at the helm just in case, there will be certain areas left alone and blocked through an electrical cafe or whatever can help defenses with technology. This is for animals as well as humans who decide to leave society who will never be allowed back in. Any person who wants back in will never be allowed as they would contaminate the society but everyone has free wishes. Children who were born outside but want to come in will not be allowed and even parents who want to bring their baby in as they are not the same as people born and raised in that society due to artificial

wombs, genetic
editing and education/
rearing.

Nutrition and healthy living

With genetic editing, society should be as healthy as they can be, each person will be given the nutrition they need. One day, with more technology, we should be able to create a pill or something to provide all the necessary nutrients to people. Until then, all food the people eat will be healthy and only related to healthy living. This is to make sure everybody is contributing to society the best they can. If people can be rehabilitated to contribute better to society they will, if they cannot, they have a choice to leave or be humanely disposed of in their sleep to poisonous gas. Everyone will contribute to all they can and I predict life lengthening techniques will advance so all the years someone contributes will be the time they have to rest as a gift for all they have contributed. After that, they can leave or again, be humanely disposed of. All bodies will be used to better contribute to society, dead bodies will be used as fertilizer or anything that can

better the society.
Physical exercise will
be mandatory and will
be done by everyone
during certain times in
the day, this will be
done starting as
children so this is
natural to them and
they will be healthy.

Values and ideals in this society

This society will have a mix of collectivism, utilitarianism, communism and Hobbesian. This society will have no money and everyone will have their basic needs met which is where the altered communism comes in. The altered utilitarianism is the needs of the many outweighing the needs of the few. This will also be specialized by every person is not the same but has different values. For example, a researcher who is close to curing cancer who could save millions is worth more than hundreds of thousands of ordinary workers.

Hobbesianism is for security and the belief that people at its core are not to be trusted

and that we need to
work above our primal
instincts to be selfish
and instead to be
selfless. This society
will be a security state
by we trust everyone
by trusting no one.
Everyone
will be surveilled at all
times for the safety of
the world and to make
a most peaceful
society with AI and
facial recognition
used. All of these may
not seem to be

connected but they are since they value keeping the world the best it can be. We need to be more than we are and work for the betterment of humankind.

Specialization, technology and space

With advancements in robots and AI, mundane jobs will be down by then like construction. Jobs that are more analytical and are better to be done by humans, will be done. I have talked about the circle where we will live. There will be certain places for children and certain places for specific types of jobs so everyone can work together to better society and humankind. What a problem in our society now is that people who would be better working or ether and would probably make more strides in their fields, are separated by nations and greed. There will be no need to worry about cost and economic benefit so people can do their best and hopefully find something useful together to help society. These circle cities will also elect a leader to represent their specializations as I have said before to represent their interests. They will have all the resources they need and will have assistance AI which will be better by having only one AI worked hard on unlike many different AI run by corporations. As we are hopefully going to have artificial wombs and with genetic editing, hopefully we will be ready to get rid of sexual impulses so everyone will work hard on their work and won't be distracted by primal instincts. If we are all working together, I predict that this will greatly impact space travel where we

will soon have
colonies on different
planets, these
colonies will function
the same on earth as
they will have certain
cities that result in
certain specializations
such as minerals on
mars or mining
resources such as
water or certain
resources is found
only in space, soon we
will be able to mine
asteroids to get more
resources which will

be used to
better society and
technology. We will
able to be will more
efficient energy
sources that will
hopefully allow us to
travel outside our solar
ustensiles which will
mean humankind will
not die when the sun
goes supernova and
that we will last
forever, we maybe
able to create a Dyson
sphere.

Language and architecture

A new language will be created that will reflect this new society's values and the way their life will be. Hopefully with genetic editing and hopefully neural interfaces, it will make it easier to communicate and learn information while also having everything at our fingertips so we

don't have to
remember everything.
The languages today
are based on our past
culture and are not
helpful to today with
being more
collectivistic and open
minded. We will have
new buildings that is a
circle which will have
everything a person
will need and will be
specialized to what it
will be used for if it is
for children or for
mineral scientists for

example. The circle
will be like the line
from Saudi Arabia.
There will be no more
roads and we will
travel only by planes,
this will be powered by
AI and will be more
like
private planes as
people will generally
not have to travel
anymore. With
advancements in
virtual and augmented
reality, people will not
have to leave to

explore but it is their right they can. Of course, each area will have security perimeters run by army robotics and AI. Certain historical places will also be guarded for us to visit, but everything else will be for the people who don't want to live in our society. They will be closely monitored to make sure their technology doesn't come close to us and

will make sure they
will not destroy our
society. In space
architecture, we will try
to make sure they are
similar to here on
earth but of course
with the different
environment, they will
have to be altered.

The way humans will look, their gender and sexual orientation

Humans may not look like what we are today and may look different depending on where they live, especially if they are born or live on a different planet. Humans will be genetically altered and implanted with technology such as neural interfaces to different body parts to make them more advanced and useful, these might change depending on where they decide to work. Humans will be altered to the best of their ability and not as weak as we humans are today. We will try to make androgynous people who are asexual and aromantic who are only focused on bettering society and themselves in the process. They might look different by being a different colour, body shape or maybe even organs. I am hoping one day we will be able to make a hive mind for maximum efficiency where the majority will decide what to do and everyone can work in harmony and do their part. This could also make us able to have pods for babies to be connected to the give men in generation chambers to advance their ageing to then become productive members of this society. If you are wondering, yes, this is based on Star Trek's Borg but no one is forced and everyone is happy to be in a collective for the betterment of society. This will remove the need for everything mentioned before as everybody as everybody will be connected and this will lead to a safe and prosperous society.

Indigenous rights and people outside the circles

Indigenous rights would be respected in this society where after we take photos and other equipment to remember and have a simulation about the former world, it will also be cleared out except for historical sites so that indigenous people can go back to their way of life of hunting and gathering. Anyone who leaves the society will lose all access to technology and technology will not be allowed outside the circles. They would have to follow the indigenous peoples rules. Only anthropologists from both sides or those wanting to study or know other cultures can visit each side in restricted settings to

not contaminate either
side but getting to
know and memorialize
others.

Conclusion

This was the world government manifesto which is needed most right now as climate change is becoming more prevalent and corporations are still producing fossil fuels only because they want to keep on making money. Nation states create unequalness between people and property and money create greed and conflict. People are also untrustworthy so we need a security state to keep everyone safe where everyone gets their basic needs and they get wants by contributing to society and behaving properly which is calculated through a social credit system. This world will be run by a new type of government never seen before until we create technology to

become a collective
consciousness which
will end hostilities
between everyone.